The Steve Romanoff Songbook

Songs written for

Piano/Vocal Arrangements by Michael Braz, Ph.D.

Arrangements Edited by Dave Rowe

Design, layout and typesetting by
Jenny Adams/Skunk Hollow Design

Published by Outer Green Records, PO Box 416, South Paris, Maine 04281.

Cover photo by Nina Carter.

ISBN 0-9638602-0-8

Printed in the United States of America on recycled paper.

Table of Contents

Dedication

To Charlie and Kay Romanoff, who taught me to love to sing.

Foreword

I have been writing songs ever since I was a kid. I remember writing new words to Elvis' "Old Shep," and being amazed at how easily a new song could be born from an old melody. My dad, Charlie Romanoff, was a natural songwriter who could write about love and life, and I was very impressed by his facility for words and music and how he accompanied himself on the ukulele or the old upright piano, all by ear.

My formal training has been limited: one year of piano and a few music courses in school. But my family was extremely musical, and both parents sang and played instruments. We five kids were singing barbershop harmony years before the Osmonds, but we didn't get the big break on Ed Sullivan. We had lots of fun anyway.

Having grown up on the old standards, I was fairly ecstatic when the folk music boom arrived in the early sixties. The lyrics were about ideas as well as feelings, issues as well as fun; and the melodies were very singable. As an English major in college, I wrote poetry and songs, but my favorite poets (Yeats, Thomas, Berryman) were either dead or killing themselves. Songwriting seemed a better way for me to celebrate life.

This songbook is the collection of songs that I have written for Schooner Fare and recorded with my partners Chuck Romanoff (brother) and Tom Rowe over our first nine albums. The book is a result of many requests from individuals, school choruses, and church groups, etc., for the piano charts, guitar chords, and lyrics to many of my songs. I hope that you enjoy singing and playing them.

About the Author

Steve Romanoff is a native of Portland, Maine, U.S.A. and is a founding member of the internationally acclaimed folk trio Schooner Fare. He holds a Ph.D. in Educational Humanities from New York University and teaches literature and creative writing at the University of Maine. Steve lives in the Portland area with his four children: Jesse, Zach, Vanessa, and Alex.

Acknowledgements

Special thanks to my brother Chuck and to Tom Rowe, the best partners I could ever hope to have, to the folks who have sung and requested and played my songs, and to those who requested that I put this book together.

Extra special thanks to Dr. Mike Braz for his wonderful arrangements of my songs for piano and voice, to Jenny Adams for her creativity and dedication to the completion of this book, to David Rowe for his diligent editing of the arrangements, to Tom Power for his tireless encouragement, to Anne Jepson for her warm support and practical advice, and to my kids for their patience while I was writing songs at night and, all too often, singing them far from home.

Teach Your Children to Sing

I wrote the first verse to this song on a sunny afternoon in Chelsea, London, in 1969. Its idealism reflects the times, for I was neither a teacher nor a parent. I didn't finish the song until 1971 when I used it as a diversion for having to finish another major project. The song is dedicated to my folks who practiced what I preach. May I be so lucky.

Guitar: C

Words and Music by Steve Romanoff

to teach your chil___ dren _____ to sing. Now, I

know what you are think _____ ing, _____ he's a dream- er, he's a fool, _____ I can't

e- ven sing ____ my-self, _____ they used to keep ____ me af- ter school ____ But if the

they grow_____ they turn to bat- tle,_____ or find some way to be a- lone_____ A- way from

life,_____ a- way from lov- ing,_____ a- way from near-ly ev'__ ry-thing_____ That gives us all___

_____ our own good rea-son_____ to sing. No it

D.S. al Coda

D.S. al Coda

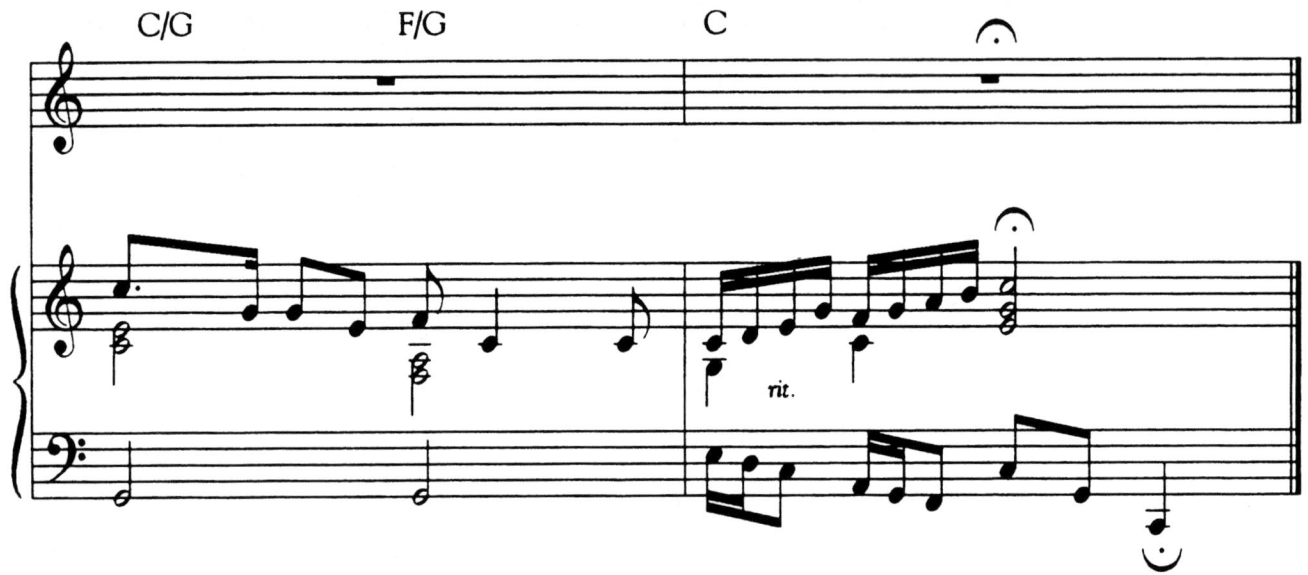

Somewhere, between your noon hour and alarm clock setting day,
If you are lucky, must be lucky, but we're all lucky anyway,
Set aside your routine pleasures for this most important thing,
And take the time to teach your children to sing.

Oh, you know it's not like working and the kids will call it play,
And as you teach them, they will teach you,
We're all teachers in a way.
Set aside your routine pleasures sit together in a ring,
And take the time to teach your children to sing.

Now, I know what you are thinking—he's a dreamer, he's a fool,
I can't even sing myself, they used to keep me after school—
But if the parent is the playmate, and the playground is your mind,
Take a lesson from the piper—kids choose music every time.

Before the fighting, or the silence that they find when they're at home,
And when they grow they turn to battle, or find some way to be alone—
Away from life, away from loving, away from nearly everything
That gives us all our own good reason to sing.

No, it won't take away your sorrows or be a cure-all for your pain,
It won't end all wars tomorrow, or bring all the deserts rain,
But if we start now with our children, while we still have got the time,
They'll be much less apt to quarrel when a song is on their minds.

Somewhere, somewhere, between your noon hour and alarm clock setting day,
If you are lucky, must be lucky, but we're all lucky every day—
Set aside your routine pleasures for this most important thing,
And take the time to teach your children—
Take the time to teach your children—
Take your time and teach our children to sing.

Steve, Zach, Vanessa, Jesse and Alex.

Day of the Clipper

I have been very influenced by Gordon Lightfoot's songs from as early as 1961 when my brother Chuck brought an album home from his college in Canada. This was my first attempt to emulate his style on a subject that intrigued me—the fastest wind-powered commercial ships. The clippers and downeasters set the records and the standards by which we still measure maritime lore. I am very proud that this song was recorded by Tommy Makem and Liam Clancy, as well as Glenn Yarborough.

Words and Music by Steve Romanoff

Guitar: A
Capo: 3rd fret

* A and low E strings are played open in the introduction.

Capo 5th fret

  A   D   A
You can see the squares of canvas dancing over the horizon,
                                         E
You can hear the chanty wailing to the heaving of the men,
        D   E   A   D
You can feel the seas up to your knees and you know the sea is risin',
  A   A
  and you'll know the clipper's day has come again.
 A   E
To the men on high the bos'n's cry commands a killing strain,
                            A
'Til every mother's son begins to pray.
       D   E   D
With a hearty shout she comes about and she heads into the rain,
                    E   A
And the ship has never seen a better day.

 E   D   A
Sailing ships and sailing men will sail the open water,   E
          E   A
Where the only thing that matters is the wind inside the main.
          E   D
So all you loving mothers keep your eyes upon your daughters;
                           E
For the sails will mend their tatters and the masts will rise again.

  A   D   A
Wooden beams and human dreams are all that makes her go;
                           E
And the magic of the wind upon her sails. A   D
        D   E
We'd rather fight the weather than the fishes down below;
                  A
God help us if the rigging ever fails.
                              D   A
As the timber creaks the captain speaks above the vessel's groans,
                          E
'Til every soul on board can hear the call.
   D   D   E   D
It's nothing but the singing of the ship inside her bones,
              A   E
And this is when she likes it best of all.

Chorus

 A   D   A
Where the current goes the clipper's nose is plowing fields of green.
                              E
Where fortune takes the crews we wish them well.
                  E   D
Where men could be when lost at sea is somewhere in between;
          A
The regions of a heaven and a hell.
                          D   A
Well they're sailing eastern harbors and the California shore;
        D   E
If you set your mind to see them then you can.
                                          D
As you count each mast go sailing past you, prouder than before,
            A   E
Then you'll know the clipper's day has come again.

Chorus

The Kingfisher

Living in New York City for a year was strong inspiration for writing a song about Maine and fishing. The melody had been in my head for years, but an ancient Chinese proverb probably inspired the extended metaphor of the king, the gold, the castle and being content with your work. The proverb went roughly:

I take my water from my well,
Fresh air from outside my door,
Food from my own garden,
Kings can do no more.

Guitar: D

Words and Music by Steve Romanoff

lone on a pier on the fore-side of town, He readies his gear for the day, In a

won- ders a- gain_____ of the oth- er men luck- y as

he. Hail to the king- fish- er,___ out in the rain,_____

Bow to his rich- es un- told, Chas-ing the sun___ when the fish-ing is done,

more.

(to next verse)

All alone on a pier on the foreside of town,
He readies his gear for the day,
In a soggy old watchcap he wears for a crown
He studies the fog on the bay,
'Cause he knows how the sky and the harbor can lie,
How the morning can promise the sun,
And how promises made can be broken once day has begun.
The seagulls will play as he gets underway,
And makes for the mouth of the sound,
This September morn is about to be born,
'Cause he knows where the fish can be found,
As the islands grow thin and the Headlight goes dim,
He points for the gray, open sea,
And wonders again of the other men lucky as he.

Hail to the kingfisher, out in the rain,
Bow to his riches untold,
Chasing the sun when the fishing is done,
Counting the kingfisher's gold,
Bringing home silver from kingdoms below,
Knowing what he's living for,
No kings of the world could do more, no more.

He deals out his nets to Poseidon below,
As over the transom they churn,
In a bracelet of buoys they're riding in tow,
And he hopes for a ransom's return,
But the jewels of the sea are not taken for free,
There's a battle that has to be won,
And a price he must pay all alone before this day is done.

The hours he'll log through the mist and the fog,
'Til the rain has decided to fall,
The calm of the dawn is long shattered and gone
As he noses her into a squall,
How his castle will fare even he will declare,
Is a matter of fortune for now,
So he'll challenge her blows, and ride her the best he knows
   how.

Chorus

Six more hours will pass 'til it's over at last,
And the sky is beginning to clear,
His nets have survived with ten thousand alive,
And his boat is no worse for the wear.
As the smile of the light eases back into sight,
And the song of the bell buoy rings,
He wonders tonight of the order of subjects and kings.

Chorus

My Lady in Waiting

I was alone in Paris for a semester of graduate school and feeling very homesick. Through the window of my room in the Foundation Danoise at the Cité Université I could hear students out on the lawn singing French folk songs. A quick Métro trip to Pigale for a cheap, used twelve-string guitar resulted in this allegory for the folks I had left at home. Glenn Yarborough does a wonderful version of this.

Guitar: G
Capo: 5th fret

Words and Music by Steve Romanoff

Ten thou-sand miles a- way and need-ing you,_____ Ten thou-sand words won't tell

But, oh, my love for you has grown From rip- ples in- to waves,___ on waves I'm com- ing home. My la- dy- in- wait- ing,_____ I'm com- ing home_____ to you,_____ All the

wait- ing_____ we've been through is fin'- ly o- ver,_____

My_____ la-_____dy- in- wait_____ ing,   I

can't   be- lieve   it's   true,   This   time   I   won't   be

leav- ing you a- gain.

gain. This time I won't be

leav- ing you a- gain.

Ten thousand miles away and needing you,
Ten thousand words won't tell what I am going through,
Married off to Fortune half your life,
You took me for my word when I took you for my wife,
Someone should have told you long ago,
Dreamers never change, dreamers never grow,
But, oh, my love for you has grown
From ripples into waves, on waves I'm coming home.

My lady-in-waiting, I'm coming home to you,
All the waiting we've been through is finally over,
My lady-in-waiting, I can't believe it's true,
This time I won't be leaving you again.

A servant to my sails upon the sea,
A captive to the wind, not wanting to be free,
Steering courses leagues away from land,
A sailor often will outrun his feet of sand,
All the silver and the gold
I would surely place in your hands to hold,
If only there were gold to give,
So I give my hand as long as I shall live.

Chorus

I've wandered in the lands of ice and snow
I've sold the desert wind to buy the world below,
Searching for a treasure I had found,
A fool believes his wealth is measured by the pound,
All the fortune and the fame
I would surely trade to hear you call my name,
The same as when you called to me,
The day we said farewell, the day I went to sea.

Chorus

The Ballad of Mad Jack

While thumbing through a great book called *Age of Sail*, I ran across a story about John Percival. His cabin-boy-to-Master story is not as unique as his controversial career. He trounced the British in Bermuda and New York during the War of 1812 and he convinced the Navy Department to let him hand-pick the riggers and builders to reclaim Old Ironsides—getting the job done for a tenth of the original estimate. "Mad Jack," as he was known to the British, came out of retirement to sail Old Ironsides to China and back for her only circumnavigation, and opened the China trade for the U.S.

Guitar: A
Capo: 5th fret

Words and Music by Steve Romanoff

land, He moved up from cab-in___ boy hand- o- ver-hand,_____ Im-

pressed by the Eng____ lish to ser- vice___ their king, As he jumped o- ver-board

____ they could all hear him___ sing:_____ Come a

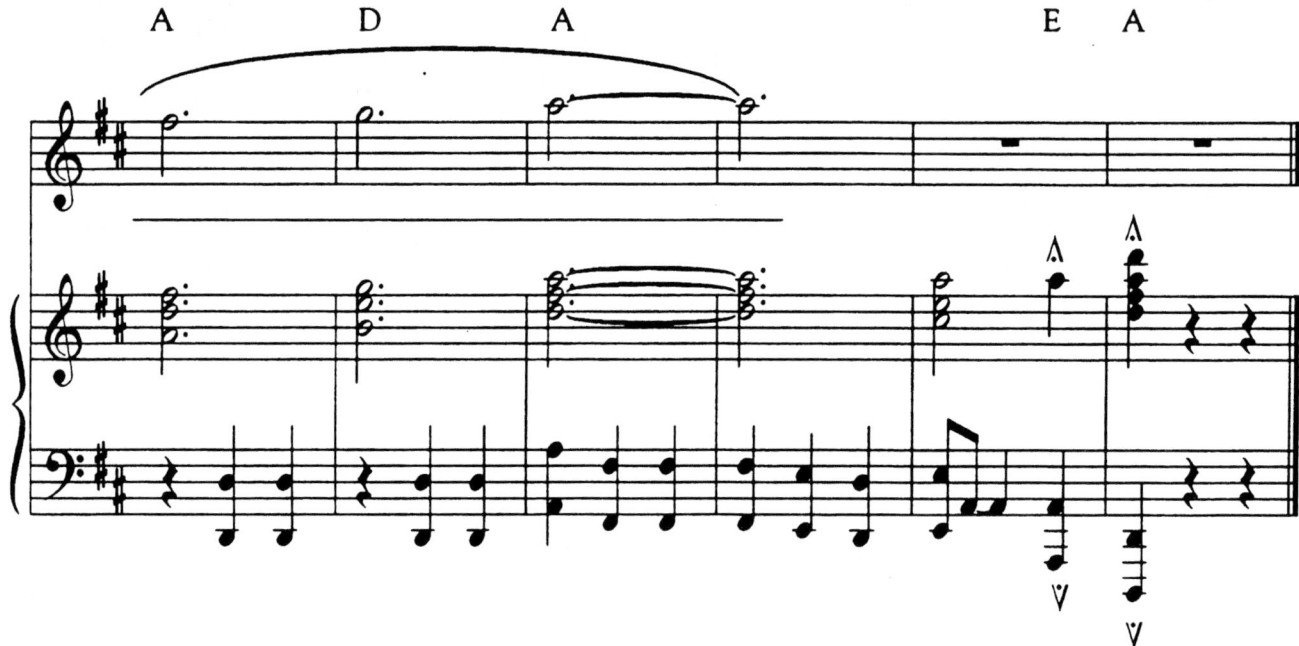

In a tumbledown graveyard in Barnstable, Mass.,
Hangs a humble reminder to those who might pass
And notice the shingle high over the grave,
That honors the bones of Mad Jack.

He was born Johnny Percival, on Scorton Hill,
A contrary lad from the goin'
He ran off to sea just to prove he was free,
and was sixty long years in returnin'.

With just nine months of school he departed the land,
He moved up from cabin boy hand-over-hand,
Impressed by the English to service their king,
As he jumped overboard they could all hear him sing:

Come a sailor, come a soldier, come a captain, a king,
If you dare me to do it I'll do anything,
I'll take up the fight, I'll even the odds,
I'll do what is right or I'm not from Cape Cod,
I'm Jack the cantankerous cuss from Cape Cod.

In 1813, Jack started to work
On a plan to reopen the port of New York,
The British blockade had everyone down,
So Mad Jack decided to turn it around:

He borrowed a fisherman's smack, so I'm told,
Put goats on the deck and armed men in the hold,
When a tender of Red Coats dared pull him aside,
His men came out shootin' as proudly he cried,

Chorus

Did you hear how Mad Jack saved "Old Ironsides" too,
From the scrapheap of flagships too old to renew,
At sixty-five years he inspected each shroud,
And promised the Navy he'd make her stand proud.

He collected the finest ship-riggers around,
From Boston, New Bedford, and Old Portsmouth Town,
He rigged her and jigged her and made her stand tall,
Then he sailed her around the world once and for all.

Chorus (repeat)

Don't Stop to Rest

Although Phil Ochs wrote such tender masterpieces as "Changes," he will probably be remembered as one of the most eloquent voices of the turbulent 1960's. His tragic passing coincided with the Nixon era and the growing sense of disenfranchisement among America's college youth. This song was to remind myself of the social conscience that drove me and the engines of social change.

Guitar: G

Words and Music by Steve Romanoff

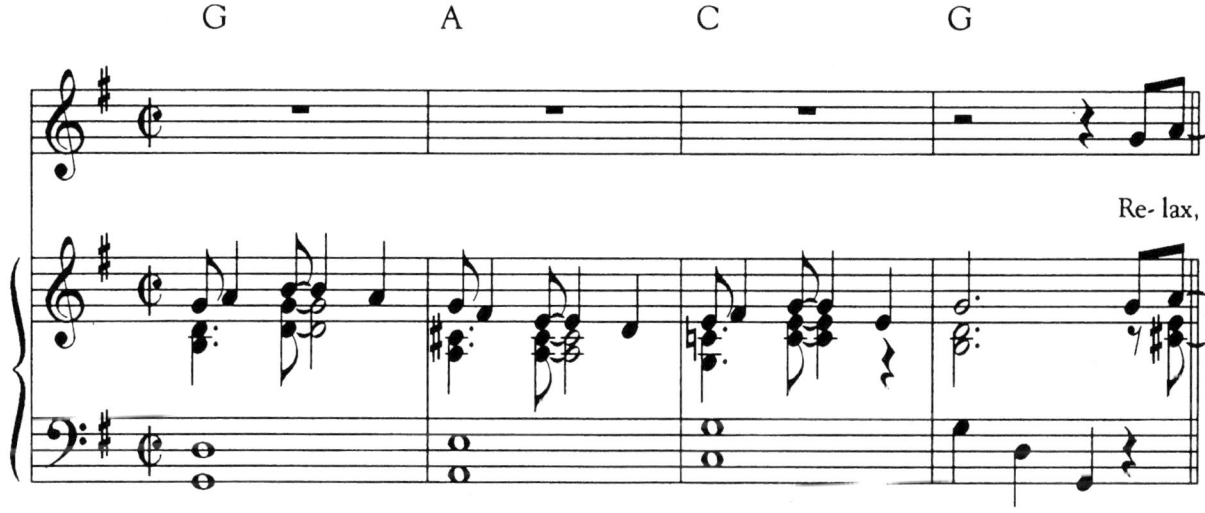

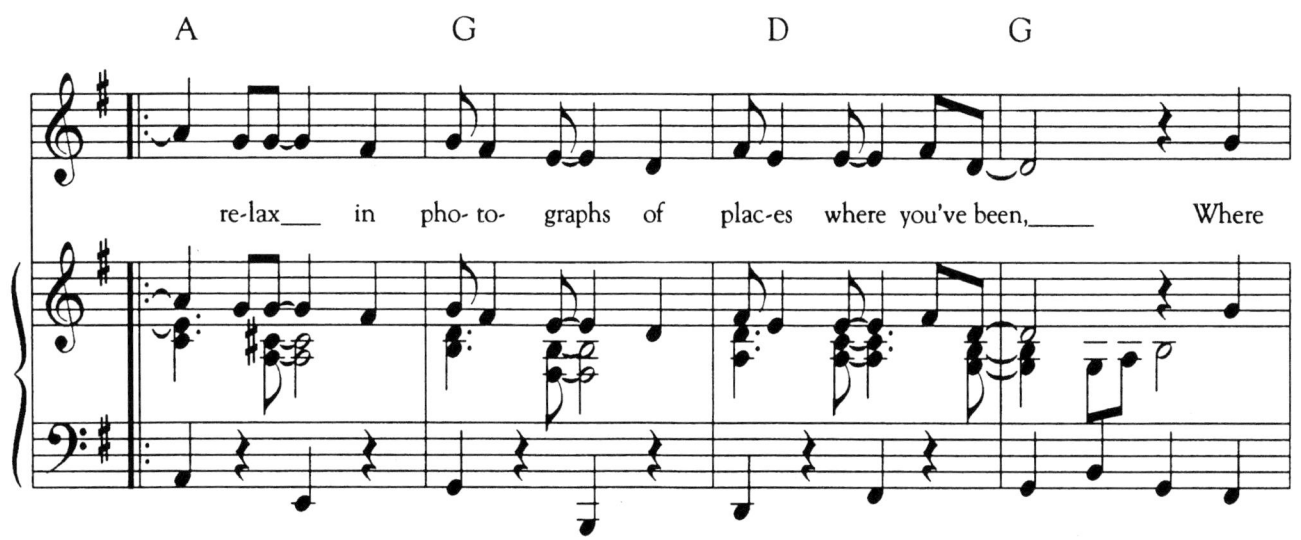

noth-ing new____ can wor-ry you, you've earned__ a rest,____ my friend, The ri- ot tears__ and re- bel years__ have van-ished__ with the din,_____ Of young bu- reau-crats__ and slap-ping backs__ and pri- zes they___ can win,_____

You've seen 'em all at ci-ty hall, you've seen 'em in___ the street,

You've seen'em mas___ que- rad-ing where___ the bet-ter peo__ ple meet,

Con- vinced at last___ those days are past__ when they should give a damn___

back_____ a- gain,___ If you re- mem__ ber then you ought to know,_____ Don't stop to rest_____ 'cause we've got far_____

far   to go.

(to next verse)

Relax, relax in photographs of places where you've been,
Where nothing new can worry you, you've earned a rest, my friend,
The riot tears and rebel years have vanished with the din,
Of young bureaucrats and slapping backs and prizes they can win,
You've seen them all at city hall, you've seen them in the street,
You've seen them masquerading where the better people meet,
Convinced at last those days are past when they should give a damn
About the anguish in the world, about the future in their hands.

You've heard the promise of the evil men
Don't stop to rest or we'll come back again,
If you remember then you ought to know,
Don't stop to rest 'cause we've got far to go.

Come all you young-eyed citizens, a story I will tell,
Of how a Great Society was going all to hell,
But children who resembled you were brought up on a war,
Had had their fill of overkill and said they'd fight no more,
It cost them miles of marching and it cost them years of pain,
Before their fathers realized their kids were not insane,
But now we're all executives to busy to recall
The days of righting what was wrong, the words of writing on the wall.

Chorus

Now don't misunderstand me 'cause I mean just what I say,
Old pledges made in passion still should mean something today,
You've done your bit, don't go and sit behind your groaning board,
And let the scrivener set down, you've given all you could afford.

Chorus

Portland Town

Landmarks are important to travelers, especially mariners, and we in Schooner Fare have come to depend on them over our years of travel. Many of us moved away and returned to Portland; we "saw the light." That enlightenment and the metaphorical use of Portland Head, the second oldest lighthouse in the U.S., was a natural for a song about my hometown. Liam Clancy of the Clancy Brothers calls it "Schooner Fare's spiritual." The Irish group Barleycorn made it number one in Ireland and it gets worldwide airplay. But my greatest pleasure comes from hearing folks sing it at concerts and hearing that travelers sing it in their boats and cars on their return to Portland.

Guitar: G
Capo: 6th fret

Words and Music by Steve Romanoff

won't_____ you make__ my bed, I see the light

_____ of Port___ land Head, I see the light,

___ I'm com-in' 'round,_____ I'm com-in' home_

to Port____ land Town. Some years a-

go, out on___ my own, I set a

course for parts___ un- known, Leav- in' be-hind

C

well ... to Cas___ co Bay, Though it's___ been

G   **D**   **Em**

years ... and years since then, My heart has

C   **G**   **Am**   **D**

brought ... me___ home a- gain. And I see the light_

D.S. al Coda

D.S. al Coda

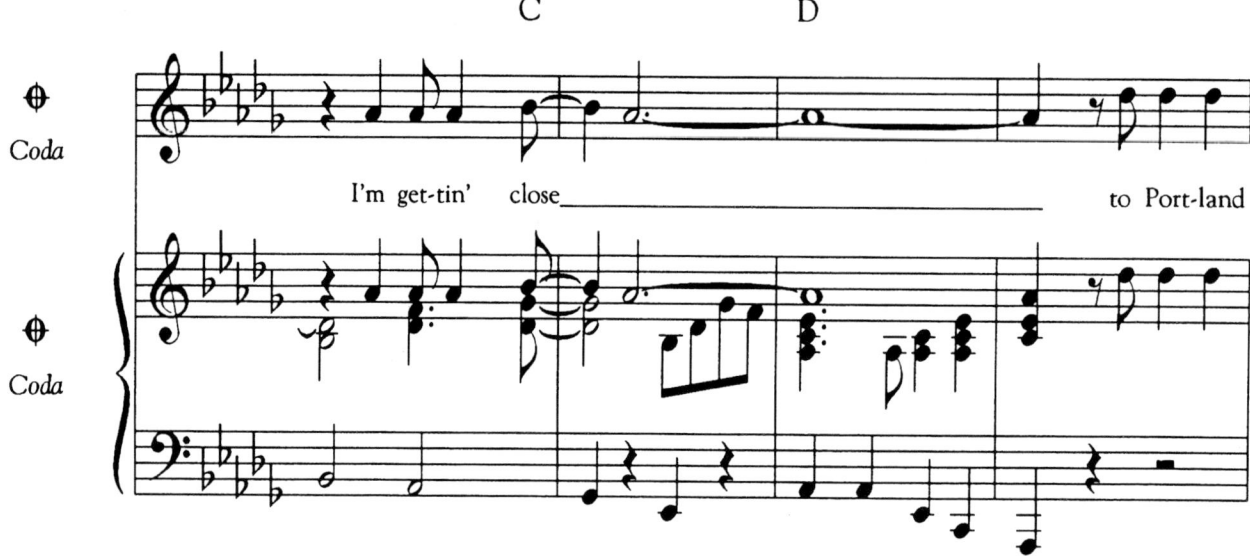

Coda

I'm get-tin' close_____ to Port-land

Town!_____

I see the light across the bay,
I see the light not far away,
And I hear music all around,
I'm gettin' close to Portland Town,
So, Mother, won't you make my bed,
I see the light of Portland Head,
I see the light, I'm comin' 'round,
I'm comin' home to Portland Town.

Some years ago, out on my own,
I set a course for parts unknown,
Leavin' behind both friend and foe,
Needin' to find what I've come to know,
As I watched the islands fade away,
And bid farewell to Casco Bay,

Though it's been years and years since then,
My heart has brought me home again.

Chorus

Of all the places I could go,
She's still the fairest port I know,
She works the sea and tills the farms,
And holds her children in her arms,
No place could know a prouder past,
Here comes the future full at last,
Here comes that beacon 'cross the sky,
And when I hold my head up high...

Chorus

My Heart's in Cape Breton Tonight

Cape Breton Island, the northern portion of Nova Scotia, rightly boasts some of the most scenic land-scapes in the world. Her proud natives, the Capers, stay on and work the mines, the fields, the facto-ries and the sea. But they often must travel far to find work; and they can be found in the pubs of the great cities of Canada taking some comfort from familiar accents and humor, and the magical music of their beloved island home. I wrote this for our McGinty friends in Halifax: John, Lois, David, Donny, Evelyn, and the singers at the Lord Nelson LBR in Halifax.

Guitar: G
Capo: 3rd fret

Words and Music by Steve Romanoff

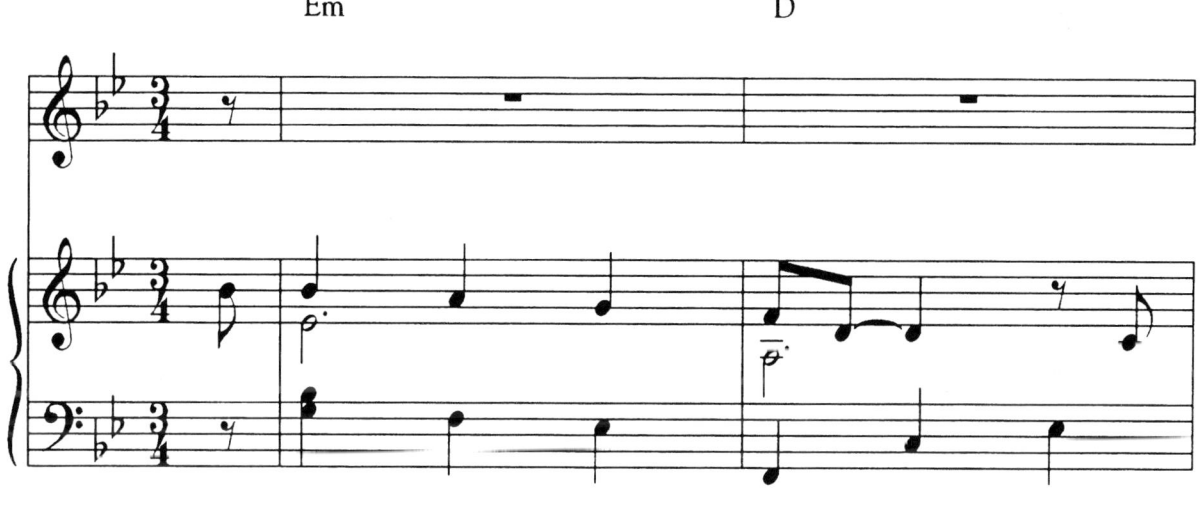

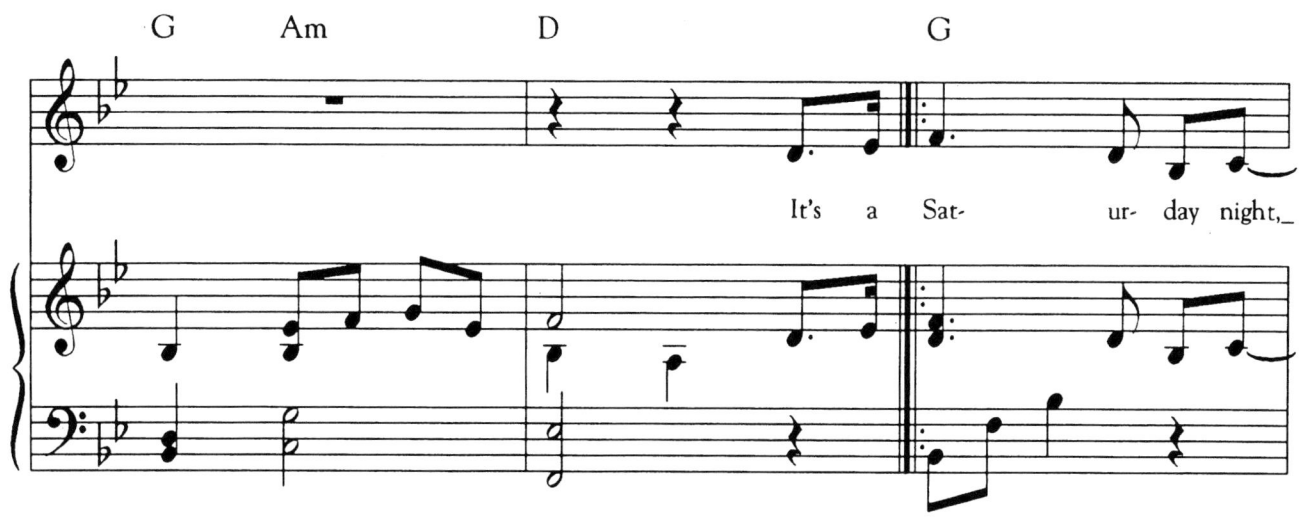

And it seems I've been out_____ here_____ for years,_____

_____ Then some- one will play___

_____ an old fid- dle_____ tune,_____ And I'll___

G   Am   D

should be all____ right,_____ Though my

G   G⁷   C

hands   hold me here   work- ing day af- ter day,____

G   Am   D

_____ My heart's in Cape Bret- on____   to-

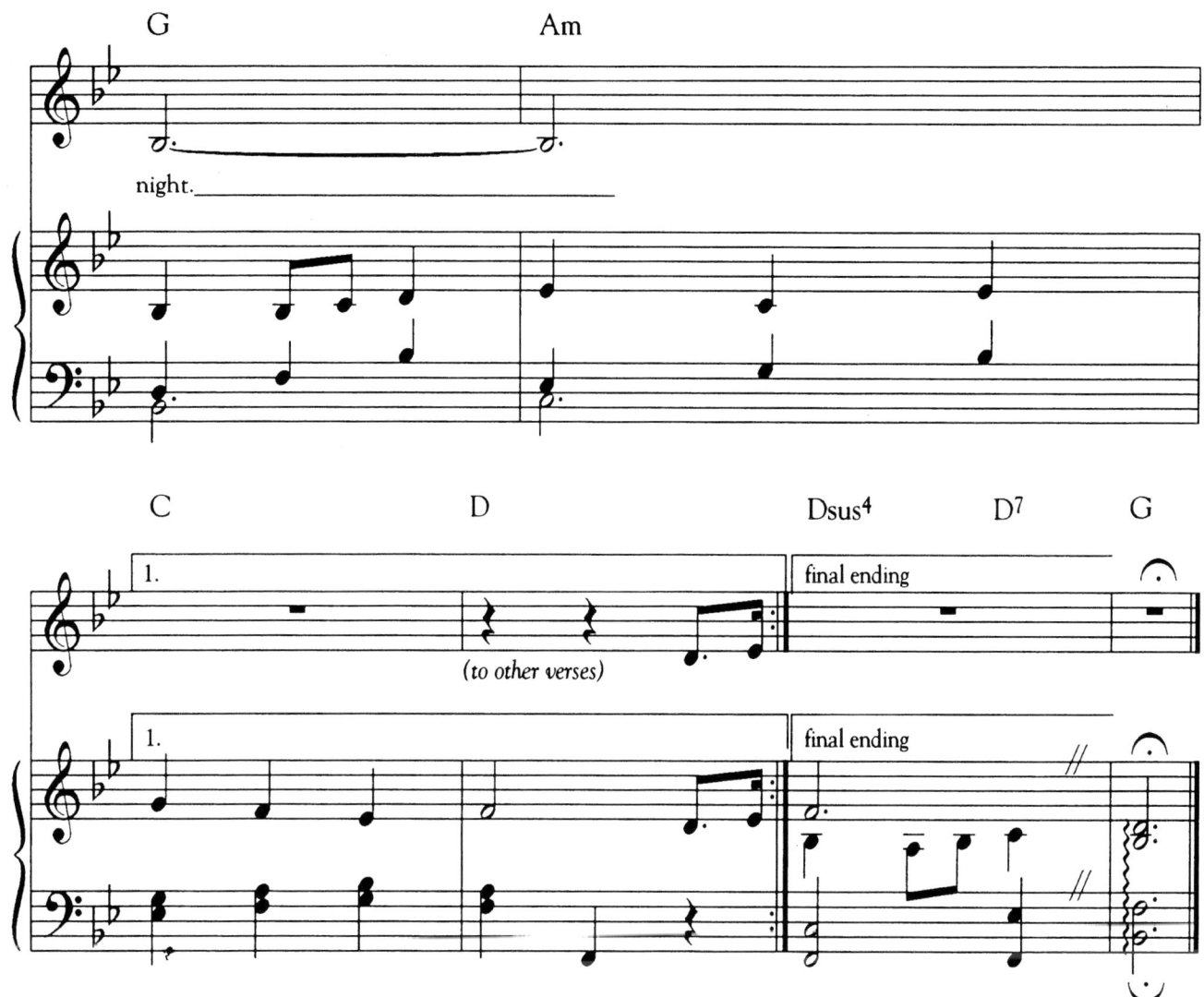

It's a Saturday night, and we're out on the town,
My new friends and me, all alone,
We will sing the old lovesongs,
We'll make toasts all around,
To living, to loving, to home,
Then I think of just how much I miss you,
And it seems I've been out here for years,
Then someone will play an old fiddle tune,
And I'll have to hold back the tears…

So forgive me my friends, if I seem far away,
In a moment I should be all right,
Though my hands hold me here working day after day,
My heart's in Cape Breton tonight.

Since I left Nova Scotia for the work I have found,
I have kept all my memories within,
Of the warm nights and laughter in Waterford Town,
Or the lights on the causeway with the fog rollin' in,
Then I think of just how much I miss you,
And how I'm out here on my own,
Then someone will play an old fiddle tune,
And I start to find my way home

Chorus

Make a Friend

In 1970, I met Jack McPhillips, a warm, hearty, hugger of a belly-laugh of a man. A South Portland native and favorite drinking buddy of his favorite great uncle, John Ford (pre-Hollywood fame, a.k.a. Sean Feeney from Portland, Maine), Jack valiantly and humorously fought terminal leukemia for ten years. His love of life and people garnered him the love and respect of his community, which honors him with an annual memorial concert attended by a thousand of his closest friends.

Guitar: G
Capo 3rd fret

Words and Music by Steve Romanoff

I once met a man___ With such a smile u- pon__ his face, That it

seemed as though__ some- one a- bove_ Had smiled u-pon__ the place, And the

mu- sic of____ his laugh___ ter, And the ma-gic of____ his smile, Was his

gen-tle way____ of reach-in' you_____ To make you feel____ worthwhile,___

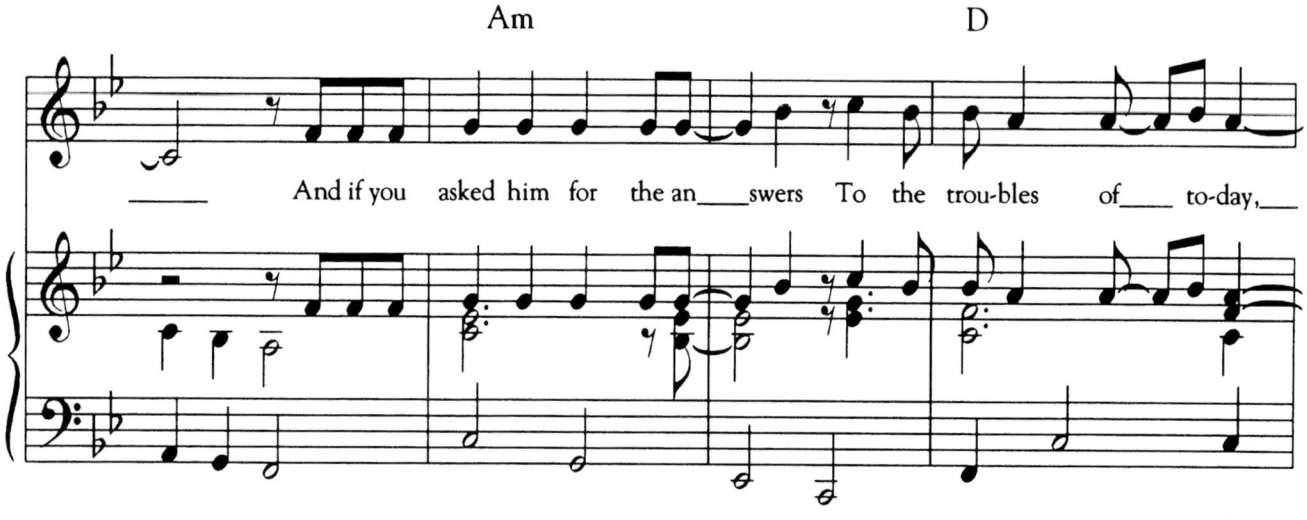

And if you asked him for the an___swers To the trou-bles of____ to-day,___

He'd on____ ly pause__ a mo____ment Be- fore____ you'd hear___ him

say____ Make a friend_____ to-day,_____ Make a friend_____ to-day,_____ Be the

D   Em

_____ Make a friend____ to-day_____ Be the first_____ to smile__

C   G

_____ in a friend- ly way_____ and if your smile is re- turned_

D   Em   C

_ peo-ple then you may_____ make a friend_____

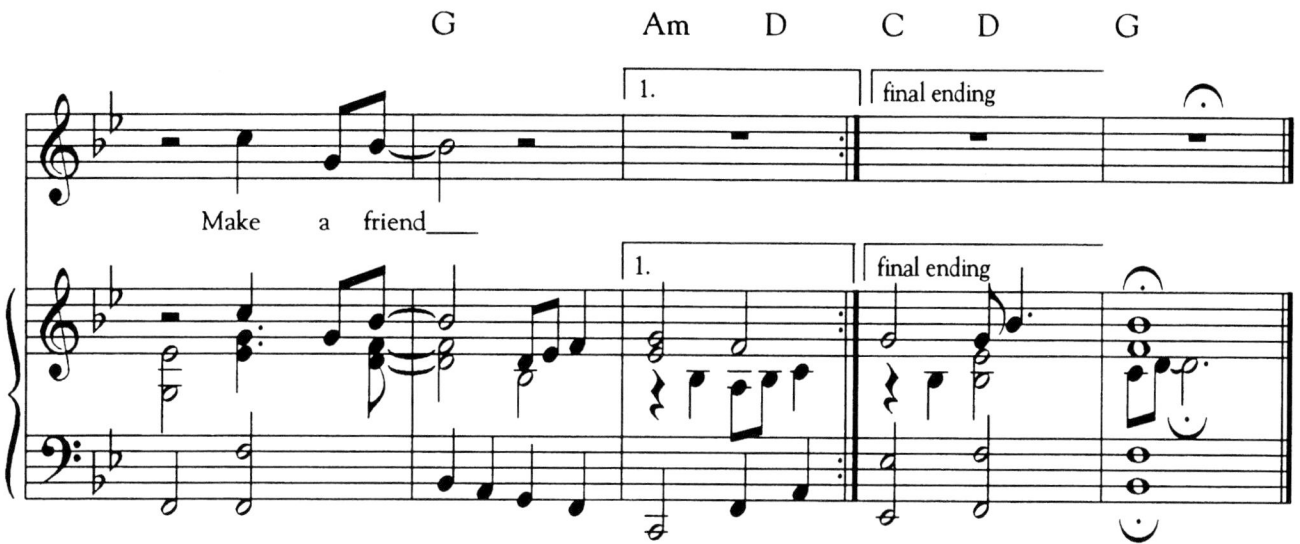

Make a friend____

I once met a man
With such a smile upon his face,
That is seemed as though someone above
Had smiled upon the place,
And the music of his laughter,
And the magic of his smile,
Was his gentle way of reachin' you
To make you feel worthwhile,
And if you asked him for the answers
To the troubles of today,
He'd only pause a moment
Before you'd hear him say

Make a friend today,
Make a friend today,
Be the first to smile
In a friendly way,
And if your smile is returned, People,
Then you may make a friend, make a friend.

Many years have passed along,
And friends have come and gone,
But I still recall that special night
And how we carried on,
And I still recall that gentle man
Who taught us how to sing,
And how the seeds of laughter
Grow to blossoms in the spring,
And how smiles grow into friendships,
And those friendships will increase,
To bring the world together,
To bring the world to peace.

Chorus

Calgary, My Home Away From Home

Our friends in Halifax told us we should be singing in Calgary, Alberta. So I wrote this song before we ever went there, hoping to be invited. Calgarians love folk music and singing about anything, especially the sea and Canada. The juxtaposition of Alberton, P.E.I. with Alberta Province was a gift of the Muse, as was the internal rhyme, even though Calgarians substitute "Charlottetown" when they sing it. We were very honored when an entire Calgary middle school assembly sang the song to us—their way.

Guitar: D
Capo: 2nd fret

Words and Music by Steve Romanoff

drift- er, but now I'm a dream- er, And it's

here that my dreams___ were meant to be,___ So

here for a while__ I'll miss my dear Prince Ed- ward Isle____ For a

chance on the plains of Cal- ga-ry._____ So tell all the folks in Al_____ ber- ton,_____ I start- ed com- ing home_____ and then in

Cal- ga- ry I found_____ a friend and

took her for my own,_____

And though it is- n't right_____ for me, To

win the land and lose_____ the sea,

I found a home in Cal- ga- ry My

home a- way_____ from home._____

(next verse) There are   home._____   If they should ask

how I'm do- ing,   I'm do-ing fine,____   If they should ask

how I hap- pened to stay,_____   If they should ask,

There's a faint silver hint of a morning,
Where the mountains meet the western sky,
And I know from the glow of the dawning sun
There's more to all of this than meets the eye,
Once I was a drifter, but now I'm a dreamer,
And it's here that my dreams were meant to be,
So here for a while I miss my dear Prince Edward Isle
For a chance of the fields of Calgary.

So tell all the folks in Alberton,
I started coming home and then
In Calgary I found a friend
And took her for my own,
And though it isn't right for me,
To win the land and lose the sea,
I found a home in Calgary
My home away from home.

There are times when I'm almost believin'
When another weary day is at an end,
And a song rolls along on the evening air,
I can almost swear I taste your salty wind,
As I fall off to sleep with a memory,
Of your green fields in this heart of mine,
A dream can go free among the fields of Calgary,
'Til it finds its way home to the Maritimes.

If they should ask how I'm doing, I'm doing fine,
If they should ask how I happened to stay,
If they should ask, say the chance of a lifetime,
Stole my heart away.

Leviathan

I wrote this song for a television program about the return of the whales to the Gulf of Maine. I was inspired by the fine book *Tales of Whales* by Tim Dietz who wrote the program script, by Dr. Albert Schweitzer who said, "...societies will distinguish themselves as great by their reverence for all creatures," and by Herman Melville, who couldn't say anything simply.

Perhaps the continued evolution of the whales is more secure because human evolution has progressed enough for us to recognize the real and intrinsic value of all living things.

Guitar: G
Capo: 1st fret

Words and Music by Steve Romanoff

Once up- on the land,_____ Be- fore the hour of Man,

Crea-tures who, like me and you,_____ Left foot- prints in the sand,_____

Through the pri- mal mud,_____ Warm of milk and blood,_____ Re-

turned once more un- to the shore,___ And to the sea for good,_____ The

humpback, the finback, the pi-lot whale__ too, The right and the sperm and the blue,__

Sing me your song that I, some-day, May sing it with you._____

Le- vi- a- than,_____ King__ of the sea,_____

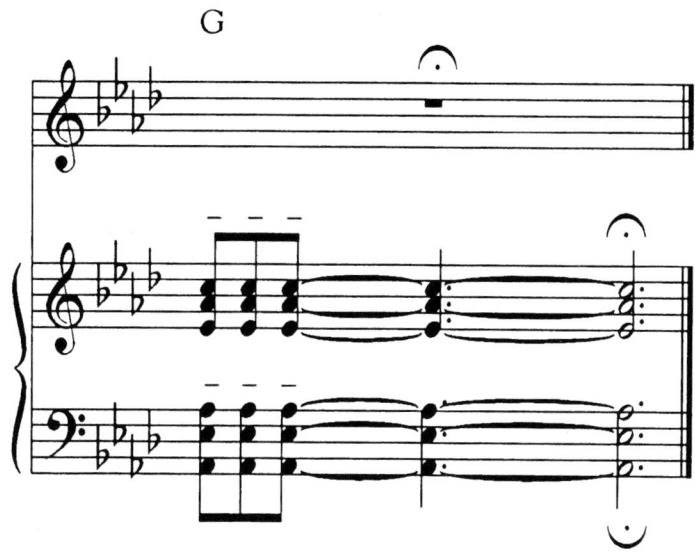

G

Once upon the land,
Before the hour of Man,
Creatures who, like me and you,
Left footprints in the sand,
Through the primal mud,
Warm of milk and blood,
Returned once more unto the shore,
And to the sea for good,
The humpback, the finback, the pilot whale too,
The right and the sperm and the blue,
Sing me your song that I, someday,
May sing it with you.

Leviathan, King of the sea,
Sing me your song and when I sing along,
You may share all your myst'ries with me,
Leviathan, King of the sea,
Leviathan, King of the sea.

As creatures swim and crawl,
Our kingdoms rise and fall,
We show our worth as kings of Earth
By how we treat them all,
From crocodile and crane,
To hunters on the plain,
We turn once more unto the shore,
And to the sea again,
The humpback, the finback, the pilot whale too,
The right and the sperm and the blue,
Sing me your song that I, someday,
May sing it with you.

We the People

The mid 1980's was fraught with confusion about what America's priorities were, or should be. We baby-boomers and yuppies were on a roll with $ucce$$ while it seemed that the least influential constituencies, e.g., the very old, the very young and the ethnically excluded, were still at the bottom of the socio-economic heap in this land of promise. It seemed that our world leaders had the weapons to wage peace, if only they had the will. This song was inspired by Edmund Burke's eighteenth-century assertion that "...governments who ignore the natural wisdom of the people will do so at their own peril." I am both proud and saddened that this song was being sung by students in Tianenmen Square (Peking, China, 8/89) on that fateful night before the tanks rolled in.

Words and Music by Steve Romanoff

D

time has come___ for rea-son to___ be_____ heard, The

B♭
G   **A**   **D**
C   **F**

pur-pose of_____ the peo___ple's what___ this dec- la-ra___tion's for_____ And it's

Gm
Em

C⁷sus⁴
A⁷sus⁴

why our foun___ders told___ us word for word_____

90

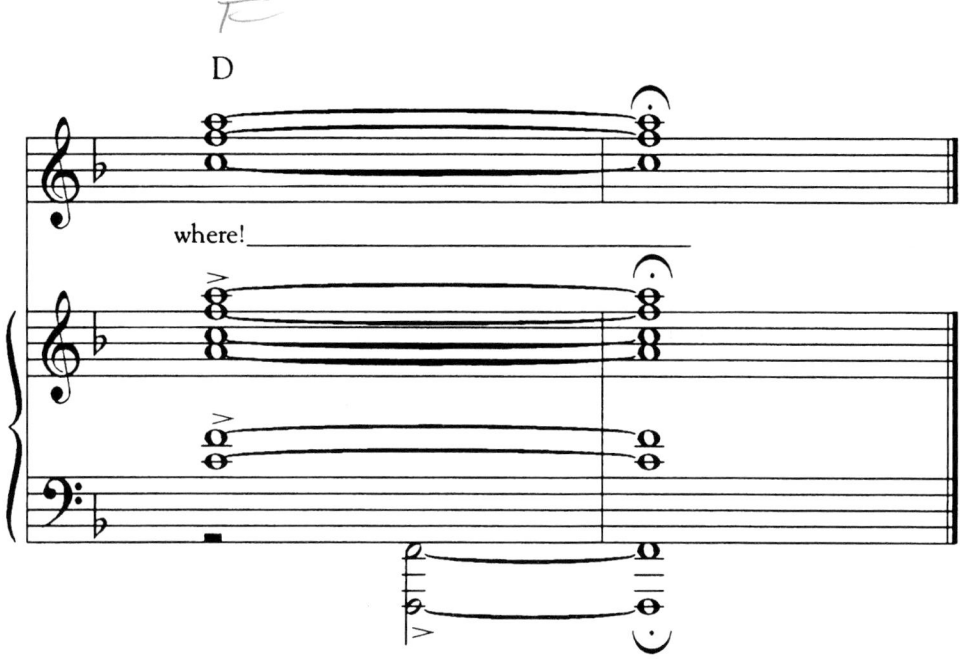

D

where!_____

We, the people, hand in hand,
We, the people, understand
That there's an answer, there's a way,
We, the people, have to say.
So send the orders to prepare,
We, the people, do declare,
Send the good news, send the word,
We, the people, will be heard,
We, the people, everywhere

There's a message in the air,
And it's a'movin' across the land,
If you listen you can hear it well, my friend,
We know the time has come
To take our heads out of the sand,
'Cause if we don't the chance might never come again,
The future is in reason,
Not in building ways of war,
And the time has come for reason to be heard,
The purpose of the people
Is what this declaration's for
And it's why our founders told us word for word…

We won't accept excuses,
And we won't accept the lies,
Of those who'd lead our nations into hell,
It's time to call their bluff,
To say to them, enough's enough,
It's time we all could hear the tolling of the bell,
It's time to feed the hungry,
And it's time to heal the pain,
And it's time to beat our weapons into plows,
It's time to hear the voices that have risen once again,
It's the wisdom of the people clear and loud,
Singing proud…

Powder Monkey

Our friend Bill Coffey was Master Chief in the Navy in charge of Old Ironsides in Boston. He gave us a tour of the ship and told us about the powder monkeys, the young boys under the age of ten who carried the gunpowder from the magazine down in the hold of the old warships up to the gun decks. They would swab out the cannon muzzle and pack in the powder. Any spark would be fatal. The analogy seemed to apply too well to anyone sent by a power to serve as potential cannon fodder. I would like to think that we are evolving away from war as an alternative for resolving conflicts.

Words and Music by Steve Romanoff

serve the pur- pose they___ still serve to- day.___
more to lose than all the angry men

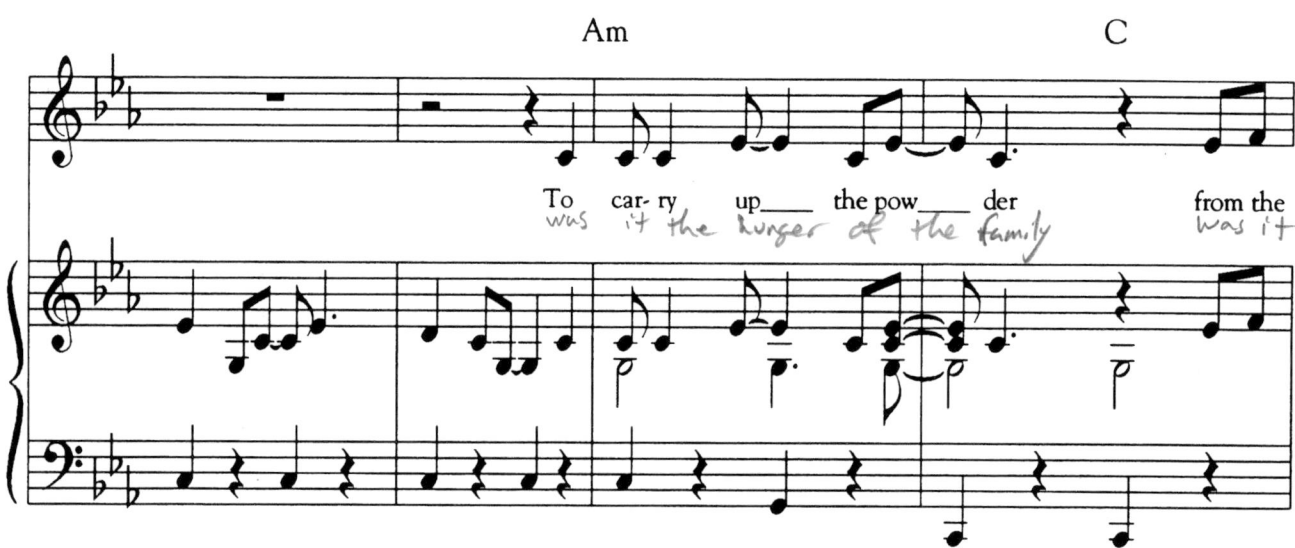

To car- ry up___ the pow___ der
was it the hunger of the family

from the
was it

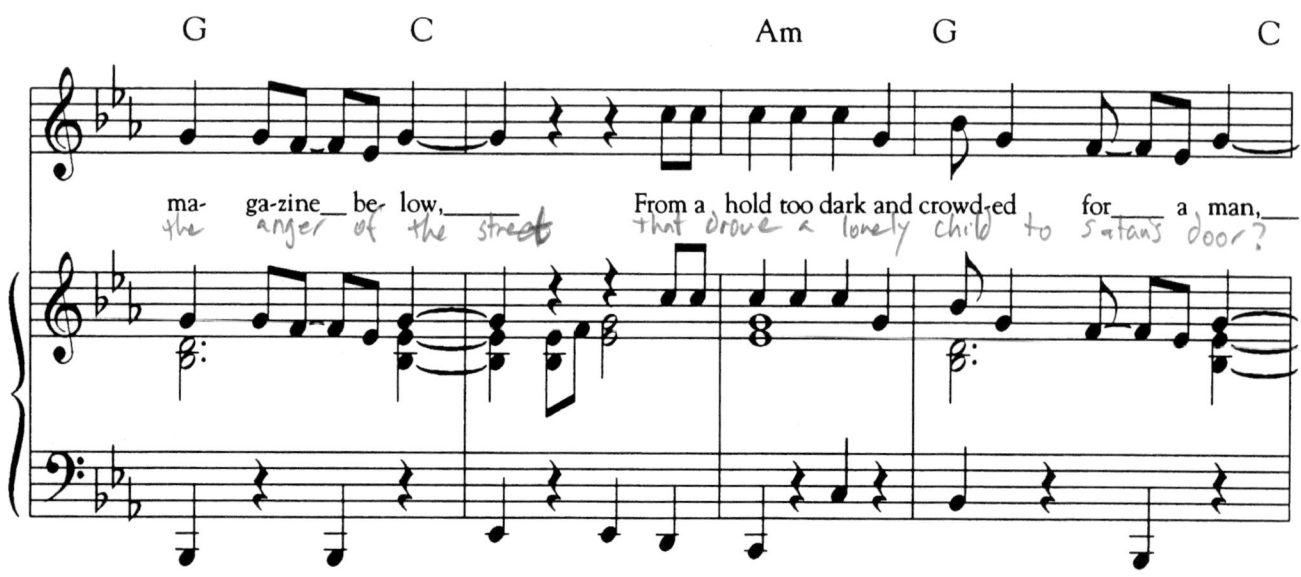

ma- ga- zine__ be- low,___
the anger of the street

From a hold too dark and crowd-ed
that drove a lonely child to satans door?

for___ a man,___

They called them Pow- der Mon___ keys, ev'-ry

where death was all but certain and Damn-

school-child ought to know,___ The price we pay___ to keep___ a prom__ised land,___

nation near complete save all for the holy innocent a shore

The price we pay__ to keep_____ a prom-ised land._

save all for the holy innocent ashore

Send for the Pow- der Mon___ key, Send him down in- to the well,___

Send for the Pow- der Mon_ key, He'll fetch us a pail o' hell_____

To keep our can-non burn-in' He'll fall be-hind the gun,__

We'll just send for a Pow- der Mon___key, 'Cause there's

more where he came from._____

They

In days of old, so the story's told,
Of boys who went to sea
All of seven, eight and nine years old they say,
To serve upon the warring ships, their captains and their
    kings,
To serve the purpose they still serve today,
To serve the purpose they still serve today.
To carry up the powder from the magazine below,
From a hold too dark and crowded for a man,
They called them Powder Monkeys, every schoolchild ought
    to know,
The price we pay to keep a promised land,
The price we pay to keep a promised land.

Send for the Powder Monkey,
Send him down into the well,
Send for the Powder Monkey,
He'll fetch us a pail o'hell
To keep our cannon burnin'
He'll fall behind the gun,
We'll just send for a Powder Monkey,
'Cause there's more where he came from.

They come from the city sidewalks and
They come from the family farm,
To trust their fragile futures to the wind,
They come from the Land of Plenty,
Through the evergreens and corn,
With more to lose than all the angry men,
With more to lose than all the angry men.
Was it the hunger of the family,

Was it the anger of the street,
That drove a lonely child to Satan's door,
Where death was all but certain and
Damnation near complete,
Save all for the holy innocent ashore,
Save all the holy innocent ashore.

— send for —

From high above the gun deck
Ring the orders of the realm,
To roll out a battle cadence on the drum,
As forward into darkness
Sail the cowards at the helm,
And they shoot the stars to see how far they've come,
Look at their sons to see how far they've come.

In days of old, so the story's told,
Of boys who went to sea
All of seven, eight and nine years old they say,
To serve upon the warring ships, their captains and their
    kings,
To serve the purpose they still serve today,
To serve the purpose they still serve today.

— send for —

Hats Off to Old Folks

Historically, the elders of the clan or the tribe were the keepers of the wisdom, and subsequently received the greatest respect in their society. Ancient cultures such as the Native Americans and Japanese still practice this.

One night on the local news, I saw an interview with my fifth-grade social studies teacher, Miss Mary Concannon. She was in a nursing home, but she was as full of life and love as she was when she instilled a curiosity in me about world cultures. I guess the bottom line is that we got where we are because someone, somewhere helped us along in some way.

Guitar: D
Capo: 2nd fret

Words and Music by Steve Romanoff

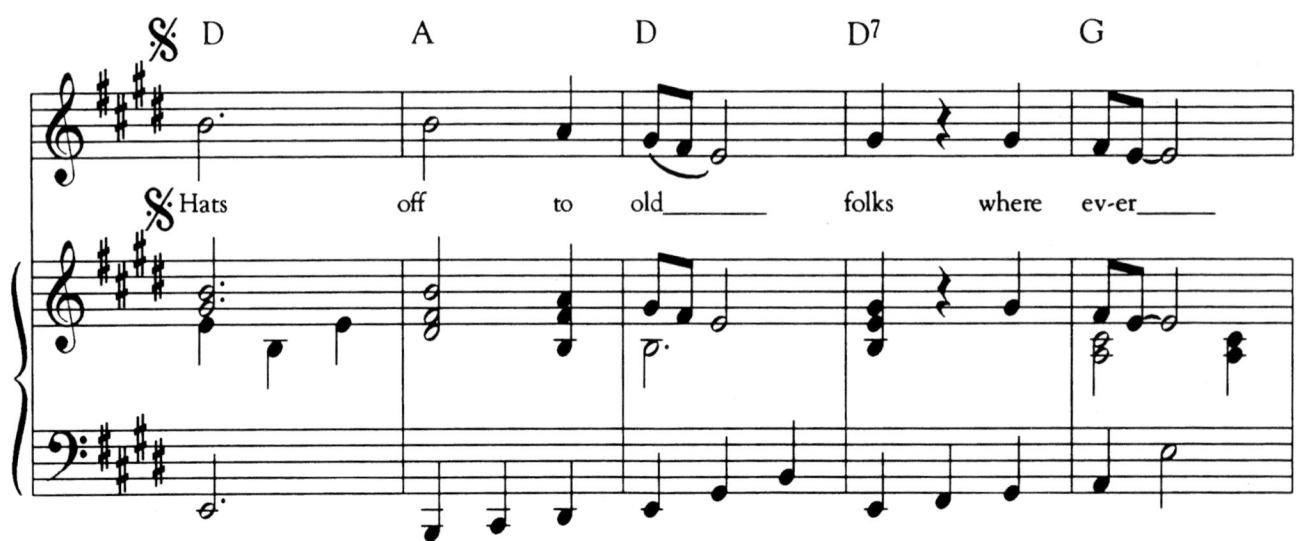

Hats off to old folks where ev-er

they____ may be,_____ 'Cause they_____ are the best__ _____ hopes for you_____ and for me,_____ ____ I stand up for old_____ folks so

ten,   he walked____ be-hind_____ a plow,_____   I

won- dered at_____ his___ wis- dom then,___   And   if   he's___

rest- ing now,_____   He   had   a wife_____   he

D.S. al Coda

Hats off to old folks wherever they may be,
'Cause they are the best hopes for you and for me,
I stand up for old folks so you'll hear me say,
My hat's off to old folks
And I hope to be one someday.

I knew a man when I was ten, he walked behind a plow,
I wondered at his wisdom then,
And if he's resting now,
He had a wife he loved so dear,
Much more than he could show,
Through all my life he's wandered there
More than he'll ever know.

Oh, see the gentle woman at the corner of the park,
Her eyes are full of memories
She whispers in the dark,
If someone were to ask her
She would tell them every word,
'Til then her prayers and stories
Go unspoken and unheard.

We all remember someone who was there to show the way,
And little do they know
They got us where we are today,
I hope we get to tell them before
They lie beneath the sod,
The value of their knowing is
The only real reward.

Boats of Stone

The New England granite trade and Penobscot Bay, Maine, are synonymous. After the Civil War, communities wanted to demonstrate their stability with the construction of city halls, museums, libraries and court houses from granite. Most of the granite used on the East Coast came from Maine and New Hampshire. Old schooners from the lumber and coal trade were sentenced to their final days carrying granite from the many coastal and island ports of Maine.

Arriving on the high tide, these boats would often dock in huge cradles which would support them at low tide until they were loaded with ballast and cut stone. Some of this stone found its way up around the St. Lawrence and down through the Great Lakes for the great city halls of the midwest. But most of the stone went south to Boston (Suffolk County Court House), New York City (New York Public Library, The Cathedral of St. John the Divine, Rockefeller Center), Philadelphia (Philadelphia City Hall), Washington DC (the Washington Monument, the National Portrait Gallery), etc., etc.

The carvers were from New England and Europe. Thousands of Italian stone cutters and their families settled on Hurricane Island and in the coastal villages of Maine. When the granite trade all-but-disappeared after the turn of the century, these communities and their unique cultures also disappeared.

Guitar: D
Capo: 3rd fret

Words and Music by Steve Romanoff

Tell me, Mis___ter, did you see___ the boats___ of stone?___

To a na-tion fi- n'lly free _____ in her new pros- per- i- ty,_____ Came a

build-ing boom for granite in the Nine-teenth Cen- tu-ry,__ And the fin-est source a-lone___ for this

Lyrics: ___ ing trade, And now I'm so far a-way from____ all that I____ know, But word came to It-a-ly____ of good work a-cross the sea,____ And you

A granite schooner on Penobscot Bay, Maine.

Tell me, Mister, did you see the boats of stone
Did you see them sailing south to honor Washington,
From these silent quarries now so overgrown,
Tell me, Mister, did you see the boats of stone?

Tell me, Mister, did you see the city halls,
Did you carve the marble monuments from humble mountain
    walls,
And great columns for cathedrals we have known,
Tell me, Mister, did you see the boats of stone?

To a nation finally free in her new prosperity,
Came a building boom for granite in the Nineteenth
    Century,
And the finest source alone for this solitary stone,
Lay sleeping in the quarries of New England,

The need for public buildings of a new magnificence,
Gave Vermont and all her marble a new significance,
And the growing need for granite on a mounumental scale,
Awoke the tiny island villages of Maine,

Through every season of the year they sailed along the Coast
    of Fear,
On a downeast course for home you'd see them ride,
Into the rising sun this schooner fleet did run,
Sailing light to make the morning tide,

To many green New Hampshire towns came this fleet of
    hand-me-downs
Having spent their buoyant youth on coal and lumber,
They'd all seen better days before the killin' quarry trade,
Now everybody knew their days were numbered,

Up to the loading sheds the leaking hulls would edge,
Ready for the rubble and the good rock,
High above the groaning sledge the shrieking gulls would
    pledge,
You'll never make a round-trip to this same dock!"

It seems only yesterday I entered the carving trade,
And now I'm so far away from all that I know,
But word came to Italy of good work across the sea,
And you gave your farewell to me for I had to go,

So here, off the coast of Maine, on the island called
    Hurricane,
I dream I'll see you again when the work gets too slow.
Yes, here under pointed trees with marble and memories,
I carve lions and liberties through the long winter snow.

You could see them from the shore always going back for
    more,
A steady stream of stone to build a nation,
Every capital and fort, the new library of New York,
Every church of every known denomination,

For the mansions of our dreams these humble schooners
    split their seams,
Like shuttles on the wind they carried on,
Some too cold to feel the granite columns on their keel,
Bound for New York's new Cathedral of St. John,

To every green New England hill where we no more will
    hear the drill,
Now the quarry men are still in peaceful slumber,
To every bust and effigy in Boston, New York and DC,
And every city curb would be too great to number,

To the hands and to the boats who cut the stones and
    pulled the ropes,
To the children and their hopes in dark December,
To the labor of the crew, their weary vessel would get
    through,
We give the credit where it's due and we'll remember,

Tell me, Mister, did you see the boats of stone
Did you see them sailing south to honor Washington,
From these silent quarries now so overgrown,
Tell me, Mister, did you see the boats of stone?

Tell me, Mister, did you see the city halls,
Did you carve the marble monuments from humble
    mountain walls,
And great columns for cathedrals we have known,
Tell me, Mister, did you see the boats of stone?
From these silent quarries now so overgrown,
Tell me, Mister, did you see the boats of stone?

Just Ask the Children

It seems that the greatest gifts that we can give to our children are love and hope for a better world in which to pursue their own dreams. This song was inspired by the great American poet Langston Hughes whose own Afro-American experience gave us his wonderful poem "Harlem" in which he asks, "What happens to a dream deferred? Does it dry up / like a raisin in the sun?" The gifted playwright Lorraine Hansbury derived her award-winning play from this second line. I have only extended the theme into a song; hopefully, a song that folks will think about and sing.

Guitar: D
Capo: 2nd fret

Words and Music by Steve Romanoff

Who will show that real know- ledge___ is love and real love sets you

free,_____ If you won- der who'll teach them to no___

___ tice the false___ from the true,_____ Just ask the

If you won-der why on-ly a few___

___ seem to join___ in the dance,_____ Just ask the

child-ren_____ what they'd give for the chance,_____

Who, ask the children, will the real teachers be,
Who will show that real knowledge is love and real love sets you free,
If you wonder who'll teach them to notice the false from the true,
Just ask the children, they're all looking at you,

Why, ask the children, can so many not read,
Why do you think there is time to debate all the warnings to heed,
If you wonder why only a few seem to join in the dance,
Just ask the children what they'd give for the chance,

Where, ask the children, will the clear waters flow,
Where will the blue of the sky and green of the wilderness go,
Do you borrow their future and pay with the interest you should,
Just ask the children if your credit is good,

How, ask the children, will we know when you're gone,
Will you still show in the balance of nature that you've overdrawn,
Did you think you could save by reducing it eyar after year,
Just ask the children, they're all waiting to hear.

When, ask the children, will our leaders be brave,
When will they give of themselves as their fathers and foremothers gave,
If all of the dreams you encourage are dreams you deferred,
Just ask the children what they think of your word,

What, ask the children, are my neighbors to eat,
What is so kinder and gentler to you about life in the street,
If you wonder whose promised delivery is so long overdue,
Just ask the children, they're still looking at you.

Chesapeake Morning

A major effort is underway to clean up the Chesapeake (the Native American name for "the Mother of waters"). I wrote this song upon the invitation of Governor Shaefer of Maryland whose Bay Folk project included a cassette/CD of original songs about the Chesapeake Bay to raise money for its cleaning. The recording includes songs by Mary-Chapin Carpenter, Pete Kennedy, Dave Mallett, Tom Paxton, Fred Koller, Hobo Jim, the Hard Travelers and others. The term "beautiful swimmers" is the English translation of the Latin name for the all-important Chesapeake Bay blue crab.

Guitar: D
Capo: 2nd fret

Words and Music by Steve Romanoff

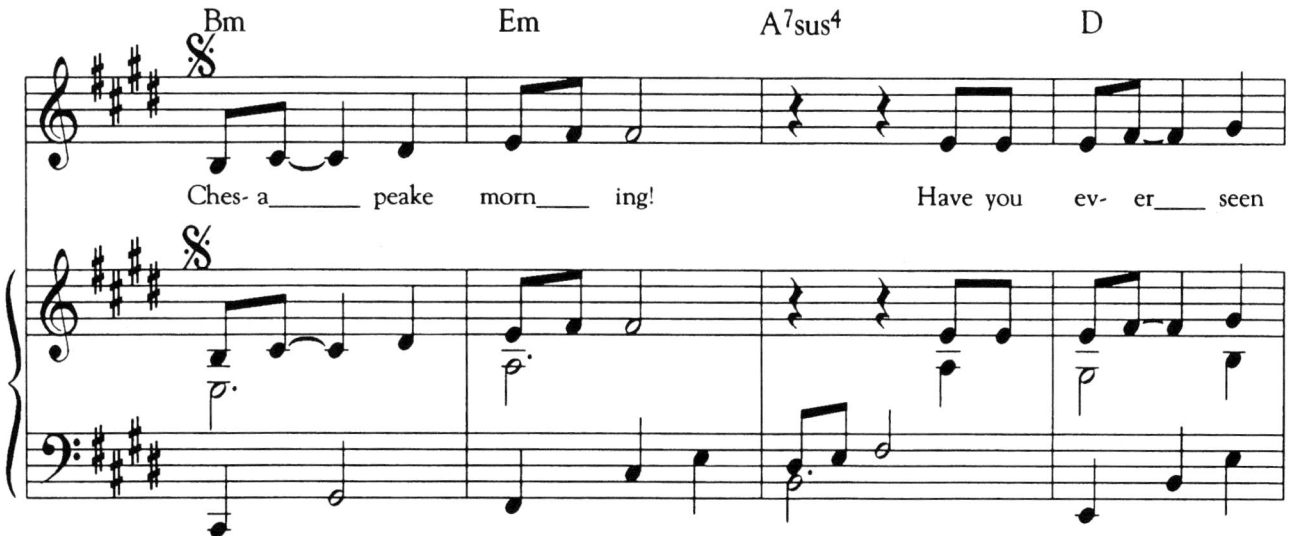

sun- rise_____ out- side your front___ door;_____ And its prom- ise_____ will_____

wake you_____ like nev- er_____ be- fore._____ Can__ you hear the a-

larm 'cause it's time to wake up! It's a

D.S. al Coda

D.S. al Coda

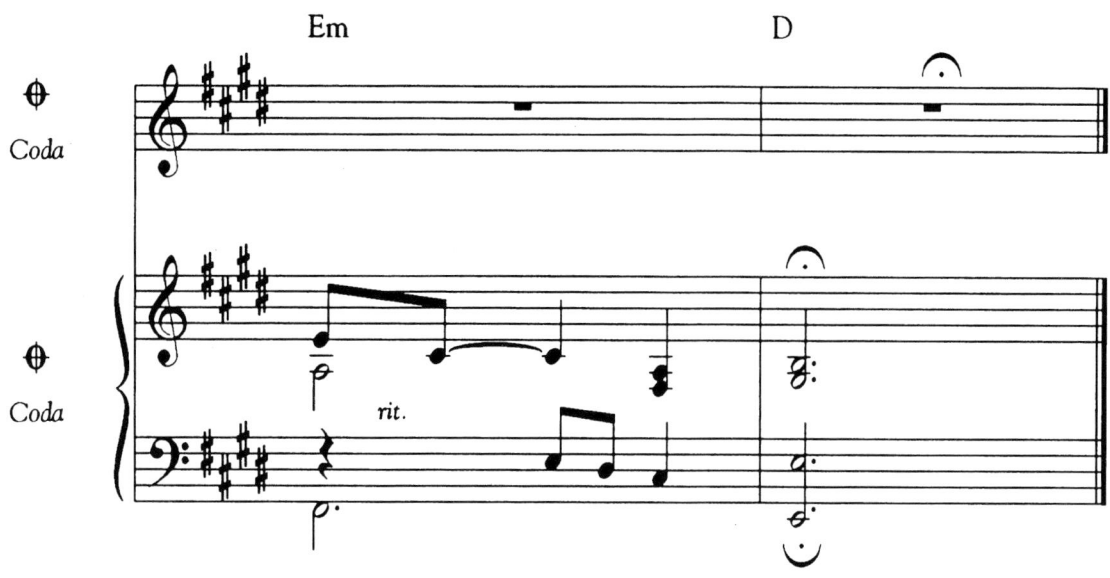

Wake up, it's a Chesapeake morning!
Have you ever seen something so new?
Wake up, it's a Chesapeake mornin'
There's so much we've been meanin' to do,
So wake up, it's a Chesapeake mornin'
Let's tell all of the neighborhood to
Wake up to this Chesapeake mornin'
And if we see the whole mornin' through
We'll wake up to more Chesapeake mornin's
And see all of our Chesapeake daydreams come true.

From the Cumberland hills to Solomon's shore
There's a Chesapeake sunrise outside your front door;
And its promise will wake you like never before.
Can you hear the alarm 'cause it's time to…

Chorus

We could work through the cities and farms on our way
To where the beautiful swimmers and waterbirds play;
'Til there's nothin' at all between us and the Bay.
It's so good we decided today to…

What Christmas Means to Me

I wish that I had chosen a better title for this song because it's one of my favorites. For kids, the holiday season holds the promise for the Day itself, after which the prizes and their anticipation dissolve into the next commercial. But as we become adults and learn to see beyond our own needs and wants, there is a different promise—of a world that, through symbols and rituals, manages to renew itself spiritually every year, and gives the gift of letting us, for a while, revisit the hopeful world of children.

Guitar: C
Capo: 3rd fret

Words and Music by Steve Romanoff

that dreams come____ true,

De-cem- ber snow_____ and win- ter rime,_____

These hol- i- days_____ that_____ meas-ure time,_____

Each pre-cious day_____ that you_____ are mine

And I___ am_____ here with you._____

real Though___ known by_____ dif- 'rent names.

find   If   we have fin-' ly   learned_____

_____ to_____ love._____

D.S. al Coda

Coda

So these are on____ly   but a few_____   Of all_

C

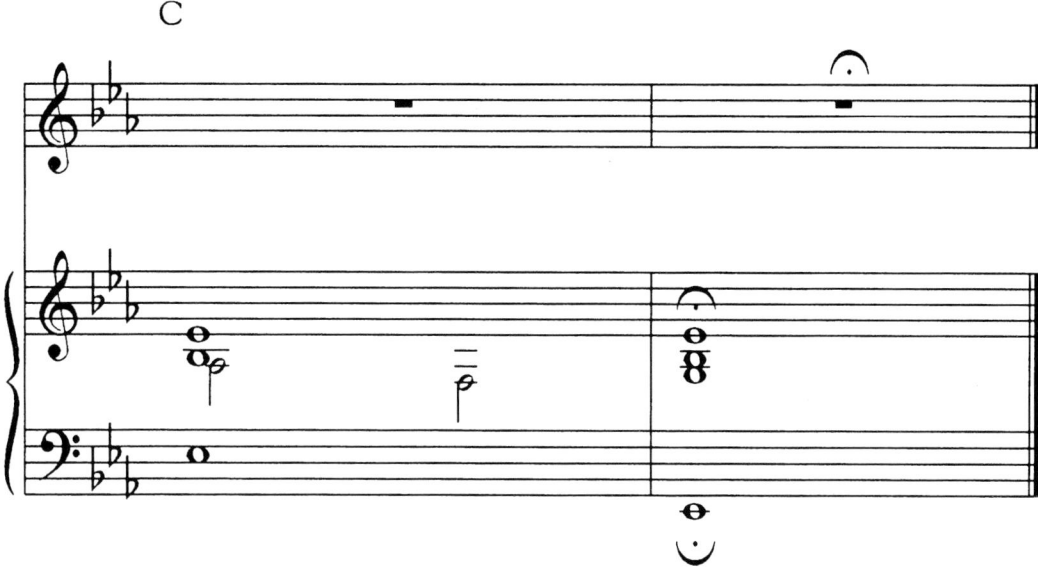

All bundled up against the chill and,
Candles on your windowsill and,
Peace on earth to those who will
Believe that dreams come true,
December snow and winter rime,
These holidays that measure time,
Each precious day that you are mine
And I am here with you.

The songs we sing this time of year,
The way we'll travel anywhere
To deck the halls with love and care
Before the friendly flames,
The way we show the way we feel,
The way we share our Christmas meal
With those whose faith is just as real
Though known by different names.

Just once upon a time there came
A message from above,
Now once a year you come to find
If we have finally learned to love.

Outside the fallen snow is deep,
Upstairs I wish they all would go to sleep,
'Cause I've got hasty promises to keep
Around the empty tree,
Or they will wake before I'm through,
And there's still so very much to do,
So these are only but a few
Of all the things that you
And Christmas mean to me.

Too Funky for the Folkies, But Too Folky for the Times

The world of folk music is ambiguous at best. Pete Seeger described it as "songs that people sing." It is a very democratic phenomenon, the result of a collective, voluntary impulse by ordinary people to remember and sing the songs that hold some significance for them, be it cultural, historical, intellectual, sociological, recreational, emotional or all of the above. It is not a "popular art" form subject to the whims of fashion and the avant-garde, i.e., something that label-dependent music critics can write about. There is no "cutting edge" to folk music as there is in astro-physics or diet cola research. The enthusiastic audience response to this song reaffirms my belief that they are the ultimate music critics.

Guitar: D
Capo: 2nd fret

Words and Music by Steve Romanoff

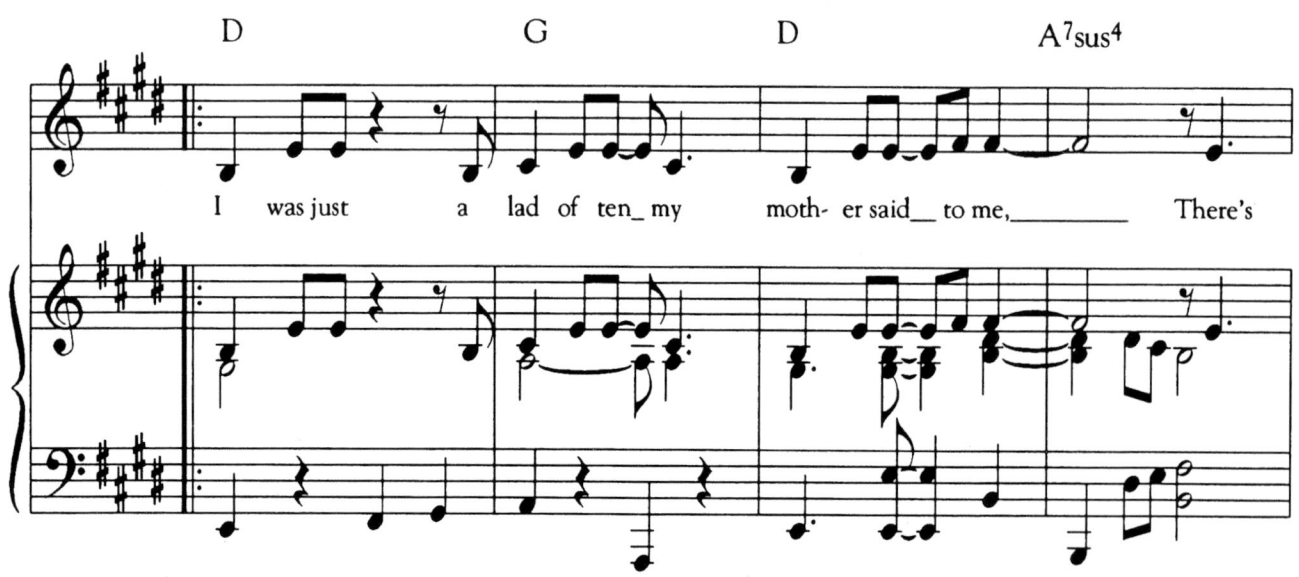

too fun for the folk___ ies, but too folk-y for the times,____ I

don't think I__ will change my mu-sic just to change their minds.____ I'd

rath- er kiss__ suc- cess good-bye__ than kiss the right___ be- hinds;_____

And be too funk-y for the folk-ies and__ too folk-y for the times.__

When I was just a lad of ten my mother said to me,
There's nothing like the singing of a song to set you free;
There's nothing like the loving that you're given in a song;
There's nothing like the magic when the folks all sing along.
So I took her for her wisdom and I took it on the road,
And for more than twenty years or so I played the best I
    know
To folks in towns and cities all across the countryside;
Dispelling rumors someone spread that folk music had died.

But now I'm too fun for the folkies, too folky for the times,
I don't think I will change my music just to change their minds.
I'd rather kiss success goodbye than kiss the right behinds;
And be too funky for the folkies and too folky for the times.

Well I got to know the business and I got to know the ropes;
And I got to know the geniuses and got to know the dopes
I know the oxymorons who perpetuate the joke
That there is something known in music as the cutting edge
    of folk.
Yes there's something known in music as the cutting edge of
    folk.

Chorus

Well I've heard of drive-through parking and I've heard of
    jumbo shrimp.
I've heard of outlet entrances and boats made of cement.
There's cold soup and hot chili and skunks without a scent;
But if folk music has a cutting edge then I'm the President.
Yes if folk music has a cutting edge then I'm the President.

Chorus

Schooner Fare: Chuck Romanoff, Steve Romanoff and Tom Rowe.

Fourteen-Ninety-One

History is written by those who own the pens, the printing presses and the gunpowder. The 500th anniversary of Columbus' "discovery" of America was a great insult to most of the surviving tribes of the Western Hemisphere, whose forebears were here at least from the last ice age. The European invasion of their world brought mostly subjugation and death, and an end to a way of life based on a deep veneration of nature. The Spaniards called the Arawaks "Indians" of Hispanola "Taino" because that was the word with which they greeted the Spaniards. The Taino were subsequently enslaved, in order to make way for the Catholic-Spanish empire. A native of the region explained to me that "taino" means "peace."

Guitar: Em

Words and Music by Steve Romanoff

deer   We learned when to grow   with the

sun   We heard all the

songs   on-ly   si_____ lence can hear

last time

148

E *tacit*   Fm⁷ *tacit*

Suddenly Fast (in 1)

E

(Guitar may play and/or double written melody in piano.)

151

We wept with the wind and the rain in our eyes
We read the stars and the moon
We learned to climb from the clouds in the sky
We learned to laugh from the loon

We prayed to the wood with the wolf and the deer
We learned when to grow with the sun
We heard the songs only silence can hear
And the year was 1491

The wind brought the wonder of wings from the east
The stars brought the men in canoes
The men brought the thunder of prayers and the priest
Their blades felled the pine and the spruce

We prayed to the wood with the wolf and the deer
We prayed to the birch and the yew
We danced all the dances of freedom and fear
The year was 1492

Love Song

My friend Tom Power suggested that, for a change, I write a song about what I feel, instead of what I think. I thank Anne for the inspiration.

Guitar: D
Capo: 5th fret

Words and Music by Steve Romanoff

I'm___ in love_____ it seems

Ev- 'ry- thing I'm liv-ing once was in___ my dreams,_____

___ All___ is well, I can tell,_____

I'm in love it seems
Everything I'm living once was in my dreams,
All is well, I can tell,
I'm in love, it seems.

I'm in love I know,
Every feeling that I have for you I show,
I don't care, I declare,
I'm in love I know.

I'm in love for good,
I'd give myself a reason not to if I could,
I can try, but can't deny,
I'm in love for good.

I'm in love with you,
It's as simple as this silly song for me to do,
Now stars above, got me thinking of,
How I'm in love with you.

Chord Page

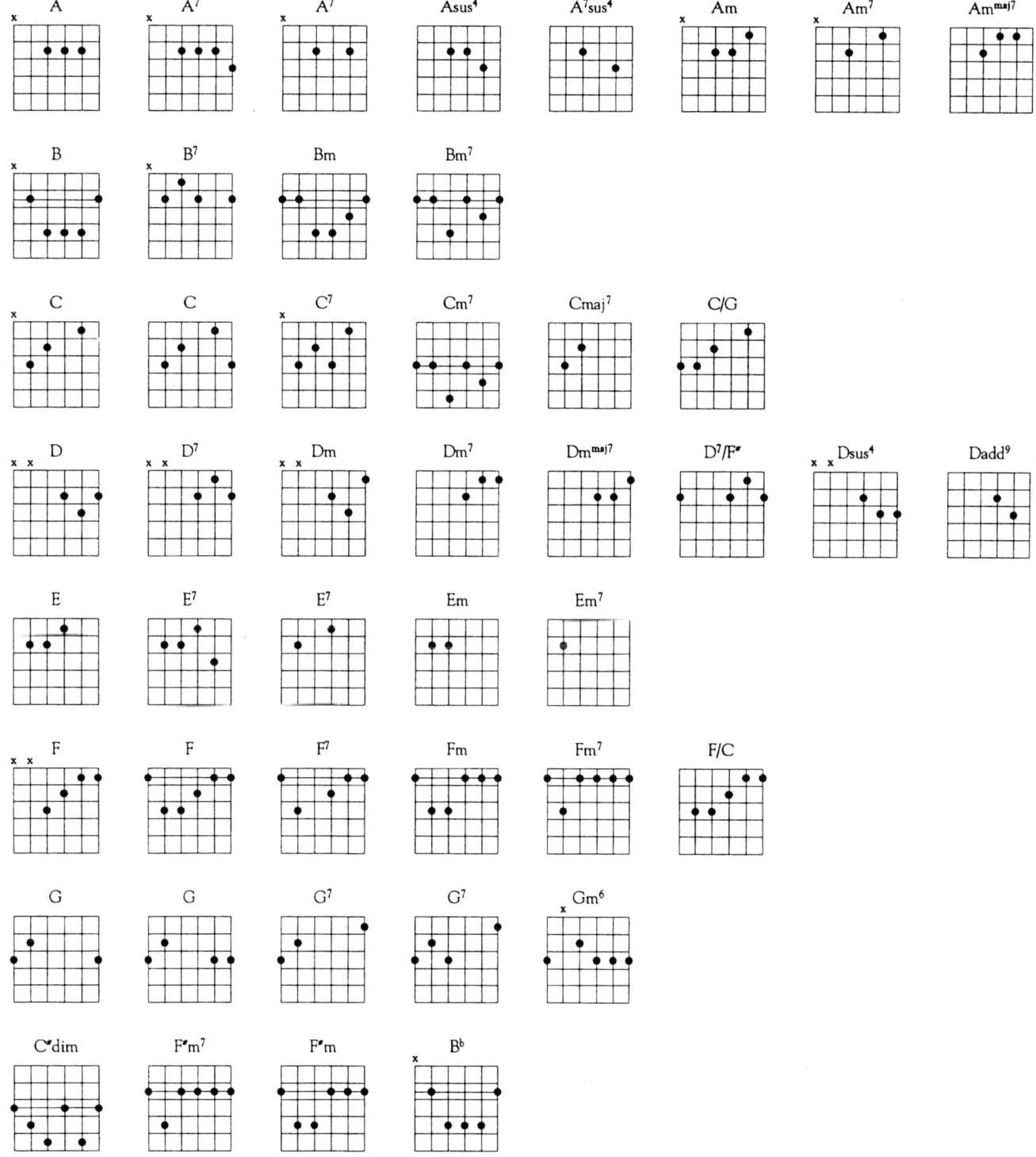

Schooner Fare Discography

Schooner Fare's recordings are available from Outer Green Records on cassette and compact disc. For a free catalog of recordings by Schooner Fare and other acoustic artists, please write or call: Outer Green Records, PO Box 416, South Paris ME 04281. 207-743-7929.

Day of the Clipper   OGR8878
Closer to the Wind   OGR8882
Alive!   OGR8883
We the People   OGR8885
The First Ten Years   OGR8886
Home for the Holidays   OGR8889
Classic Schooner Fare   OGR8891
Signs of Home   OGR8893
For the Times   OGR8909

Available on video:

Schooner Fare In Concert   OGR8903